Tonight in the Palace

Andrew McDonough

It was late at night and all the sheep
were in their beds and fast asleep.
They snuggled up, while Cecil snored . . .

when out of heaven, an angel soared.

"Wake up, sheep! Wake up!" he said.
"Stop yer dreamin', get out of bed.
Listen, sheep, good news I bring.
In Bethlehem is born a king!
He's cute, he's cuddly,
he's nine pound ten.
So what are you waiting for?
Visit him then!"

Visit the king! This'll be fine,
tonight in the palace we're going to dine.
We'll start with pavlova, then peacock eggs fried,
with fancy fresh mushrooms piled up on the side.
Load up on lobster, dunk in the dips,
bypass the salad and pig out on chips,
then finally finish with a small minty thing,
that's what you eat in the house of the king!

With stomachs rumbling, they leapt out of bed,
charged over the hill and then Cecil said,

Visit the king! Way to go!
Royalty throw a spectacular show!
There'll be jugglers 'n' jesters and gymnasts galore,
sword swallowers, fire eaters, but wait there's more!

Trev and the Bad Boys blasting out tunes
while deadly dirt bikes are ridden by hoons.
Then fireworks shot from the boat in the moat
'cos that's how a king gets the popular vote.

Down the Bethlehem road they run at a trot
when Cecil yells out, "Hey fellas, guess what!"

Visit the king, this'll be neat!
Think of the people we're going to meet!
The Belgian ambassador, the Sultan of Malta,
the Olympic swim team, and a pole vaulter!

We'll dance the night away with Princess Natasha.
She's style, she's elegance, an absolute smasher.
With the beautiful people we'll be ming-el-ing
that's who you meet in the house of the king!

Down the Bethlehem road, around all the bends,
when Cecil called out to all of his friends,

Visit the king! This'll be ace!
Kings always live in a big fancy place!
We'll slide down the banisters, swing from the drapes,
splash in the bath, swim in the lakes,
slouch in the bean bags, skate down the hall,
sneak out the back, then when we've done it all . . .

sleep in four poster beds with plenty of spring,
that's where one sleeps in the house of the king!

But in Bethlehem, they wandered around,
the king, and his palace, nowhere to be found.
Then Meredith said "Here's some suggestions,
let's, go to the pub . . .
and ask for directions!"

The publican listened to what the sheep said,
scratched at his beard, then shook his head,
"I don't know no palace, an' I don't know no king.
But that Princess Natasha's a pretty young thing.
We don't do pavlova, besides you're too late,
we've run outta schnitzel, chef knocked off at eight.
I ain't got no room, an' I ain't got no bed.
Heck, the last lot that rocked up, I shoved in the shed."

Visit the king, why'd we come all this way?
Let's head out to the back and crash on the hay.

Out in the shed was this bloke and a lady.
There goes our sleep, she's holding a baby!
Those things grizzle and howl and cry — but then . . .
he's cute, he's cuddly,
he's nine pound ten.

The Back Page

Tonight in the Palace is based on the account of Jesus' birth in Luke 2:8-20. Everyone knows that baby kings are born in a royal palace! Well, that's what Cecil and his friends thought! But to their amazement they discovered that Jesus, the greatest king ever, was born in humble surroundings. Cecil may not have eaten pavlova, seen the royal jugglers or danced with Princess Natasha but he's not complaining. He met the king and Cecil wouldn't swap that for anything!

Before the story

Begin by asking,
"If you were going to visit a king, what would you look forward to the most?"
I'm sure your child will have a long list of exciting things to share. Then you can say,
"Let me tell you a story of some friends and their excitement at the thought of visiting a king."

Read the story

After the story

You may like to ask if they know who the baby king is and when we celebrate his birthday.

Christmas is a time of excitement and anticipation for sheep and your children. Some of us get excited about jugglers and jesters, others about pavlova and presents. These things are all fantastic but the best thing about Christmas is the birth of Jesus the King who brings life and hope. What was Good News at the first Christmas is still the Good News today!

God's blessing,
Andrew

Luke 2:8—20 (CEV)

That night in the fields near Bethlehem some shepherds were guarding their sheep. All at once an angel came down to them from the Lord, and the brightness of the Lord's glory flashed around them. The shepherds were frightened. But the angel said, "Don't be afraid! I have good news for you, which will make everyone happy. This very day in King David's hometown a Saviour was born for you. He is Christ the Lord. You will know who he is, because you will find him dressed in baby clothes and lying on a bed of hay."

Suddenly many other angels came down from heaven and joined in praising God. They said:

"Praise God in heaven!
Peace on earth to everyone who pleases God."

After the angels had left and gone back to heaven, the shepherds said to each other, "Let's go to Bethlehem and see what the Lord has told us about." They hurried off and found Mary and Joseph, and they saw the baby lying on a bed of hay.

When the shepherds saw Jesus, they told his parents what the angel had said about him. Everyone listened and was surprised. But Mary kept thinking about all this and wondering what it meant.

As the shepherds returned to their sheep, they were praising God and saying wonderful things about him. Everything they had seen and heard was just as the angel had said.

Title: Tonight in the Palace
ISBN: 9781921229411

Published edition © 2010 Lost Sheep Resources Pty Ltd
Text and illustrations © 2010 Andrew McDonough

The Bible text is from The Bible for Today (Contemporary English Version) © American Bible Society 1991, 1995. Used by permission of the Bible Society Australia GPO Box 4161, Sydney NSW 2001.

First printing September 2010

31 30 29 28 27 26 25 24 23 22   10 9 8 7 6

A catalogue record for this work is available from the National Library of Australia.

Trev and the Bad Boys' bass player: Sam Pearce
Princess Natasha's stylist: Simon Pearce

If you plan to recreate the banquet in this book for your Christmas dinner, we expect to be invited.

Designed and published by Lost Sheep
Distributed by Koorong in partnership with Lost Sheep
Printed in Australia by Finsbury Green
Koorong Books Pty Ltd, 28 West Parade, West Ryde, NSW 2114 Australia
Lost Sheep, PO Box 3191, Unley SA 5061, Australia
info@lostsheep.com.au
lostsheep.com.au

printed
carbon
neutral

225kg
CO2 saved
on this project